FOCUS:
Creating Career + Brand Clarity – 2nd Edition

Danielle Beauparlant Moser
+ Debra Fehr Heindel

CareerWise Publishing

Fort Worth, Texas

CareerWise Publishing
Fort Worth, Texas, USA 76244
www.careerwisepublishing.com

Publisher's Note: The author and publisher have made every attempt to provide the reader with accurate, timely, and useful information. The information presented here is for reference purposes only. The author and publisher make no claims that using this information will guarantee the reader a job. The author and publisher shall not be liable for any losses or damages incurred in the process of following the advice of this book.

FOCUS: Creating Career + Brand Clarity / Moser and Heindel. -- 2nd ed.
ISBN-13: 978-0692868836 (CareerWise Publishing)
Cover: Morgan B. Shook

Dedication

This book is dedicated to our families - with love and thanks for their ongoing support and continuing patience.

And to our clients who gave us feedback and helped us through these many years as we designed, tested, and refined the strategies and exercises laid out in this book. Your success has been our success.

— DBM + DFH

"The only way to do great work is to love what you do. If you haven't found it yet, keep looking. Don't settle."

- Steve Jobs

"Where your talents and the needs of the world cross; there lies your vocation."

- Aristotle

CONTENTS

INTRODUCTION

The reality of the global job market (which is shifting to more of a gig economy) is that the emphasis has changed from 'lifetime employment' where the employer was in control to you being in control. That is, creating your own sustainable employability.

For many, this is a paradigm shift in the way you think about and actively manage your career. In other words, when it comes to **your** career, you need to think and act like an entrepreneur.

Sustainable employability is largely about strategy. Proactive career management is more than just doing a good job at work or writing a good résumé/CV. It's about identifying your next-best-step:

– Managing your employability -- keeping an eye on the bigger picture to ensure your skills and expertise are marketable and in-demand -- not just now, but in the future as well.

– Balancing your work life, making informed decisions, and reinventing yourself on your terms, not someone else's.

– Making sure your messaging resonates with your target audience and hooks them into wanting to talk to you -- as that conversation is the decision-making point.

In other words, when you identify your next-best-step, it's about finding a role and an environment in which you can be successful and flourish: loving what you do, being appreciated, and ultimately being your best self at work.

To drill it down to the more tactical level, it's not about how you craft the perfect résumé/CV or LinkedIn profile; it's about having a clear focus, understanding the strategy of marketing yourself, and developing an on-target message (i.e. brand).

Perhaps you're ahead of the curve and picked up this book to take a proactive step to better manage your career. Perhaps you've been affected by the recession and find yourself only now taking steps to ensure your employability. Or maybe, you've decided to reinvent yourself and finally do what you want to do.

Whatever the circumstances, this book was written specifically for people desiring to take control of their own employability and find meaning and purpose in their work.

We call that finding your "*Flourish Factor*" because, let's face it, when your work life stinks, it can have a profoundly negative affect on the other areas of your life. Wouldn't you agree: the world would be a better place if we all flourished at work?

THE FLOURISH FACTOR STORY

People often ask us where the idea for the *Flourish Factor* originated. It all started when Debra and her husband purchased a previously owned home in Northern California.

On the back patio, the prior owners had left behind a pine tree in a planter. It was a perfectly fine little pine tree. It was green; it was growing; it was healthy. After moving the pine tree around on the patio for a few years, Debra decided she wanted to plant it in the backyard.

Source: iselinursery.com

Over the course of the next year, the pine tree grew at twice its normal rate -- flourishing in its new environment.

It was then that Debra realized that people are just like that pine tree. There are environments in which we can exist and survive, but in the right environment we can actually *thrive* and flourish.

When she shared the story with Danielle, they realized what a fitting metaphor it was for the research they were completing for this book. Thus, was born the idea of the *Flourish Factor* Profile.

CAREER OPTIONS

Often when we work with clients, one the first things that happens is they feel overwhelmed about what comes next.

Usually, that's because they're getting their identity from online postings -- the jobs that are immediately available and would generate income.

The problem is, with so many posted openings for jobs, it becomes even more confusing.

That's where our Career Management Diagnostic can help. The diagnostic will identify:

– Your Flourish Factor,

– A path to your next-best-step, and

– The strategy to manage your own sustainable employability.

PART ONE:
Creating Career Clarity

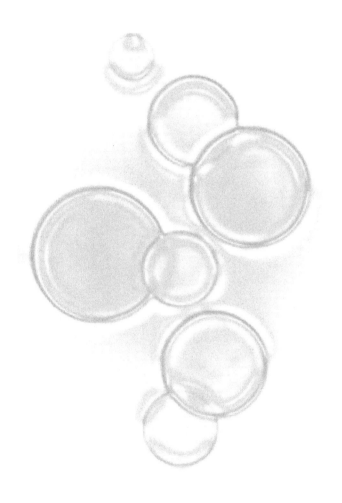

1. Introducing the Career Management Diagnostic

You've heard it said that the hardest part in any work is getting started. Good news. When you picked up this book and read this far, you took that first step!

The rest is much easier than you may think. It is a matter of collecting as much information about you and the marketplace as you can, and recording it in such a way that you can practically and logically access it later. You are the only person who has the necessary information.

The intention of this diagnostic is to help make the career management process more approachable, manageable, and less nebulous. From an efficiency perspective, the diagnostic will clarify **what you do know,** so you can direct your attention to **researching and answering the questions to which you don't yet have answers.**

When considering any next step in your career, especially one that's going to allow you to be your best professional self (and determine your *Flourish Factor*), it's critical to answer these 3 questions:

1) What do I want to do? (Note, it's not the same as "What can I do?") It's really about where you're at your best, because that is where you are the most marketable.

2) How will my personal priorities impact my next step? Examples: financial requirements or geography.

3) What's the profile of the organization and who is the ultimate stakeholder who is losing sleep over the issue for which I add the most value?

These 3 questions must be answered in context of the other. None of them can stand in isolation. The question, "What do I want to do?" isn't a pie-in-the-sky- question because it must be answered in the context "Who needs what I have?" – in other words, the demands of the marketplace.

For instance, aspiring to be a flying unicorn will only be a viable option if there is a market demand for flying unicorns.

Source: animals09890.deviantart.com

Whatever that step is, it should be your best-next-step. This career management diagnostic will help you determine where you need to spend your time gathering the decision-grade data that will allow you to move forward.

All 3 of these questions need to be answered if you're considering any of the following options:

- An internal promotional opportunity (often called career mobility)

- A move outside your current organization

- A complete career / personal re-invention

- Options for the 2nd half of your career (i.e. retiring 'actively')

- Entrepreneurial options

As we explore each question more fully, please note that this diagnostic serves as the framework for the book. All but one of the exercises is framed under the question(s) you might need help answering.

Our goal is that this tool will help you quickly diagnose what-you-already-know versus what-you-need-to-know so you can focus your efforts more efficiently.

To be clear, our goal is to help you use these questions to ultimately create the picture of where you are your **best-self** -- your *Flourish Factor*.

Question 1: What do I WANT to do?

As we explore the question **"What do I want to do?"** note, it's not asking about all the things you can do. That's not the same question. It's about **where you're at your best**, because that is where you are the **most marketable**.

There are many things you **can do**, but just because you can do something doesn't mean that you want to do it. Or, that it's something at which you excel.

Although there are many ways to help you separate "what you can do" from "what you really want to do," a simple way to start is with the exercises in Chapter Two, *Career Management Diagnostic Question 1: What do I Want to do?*

Question 2: How will my personal priorities impact my next step?

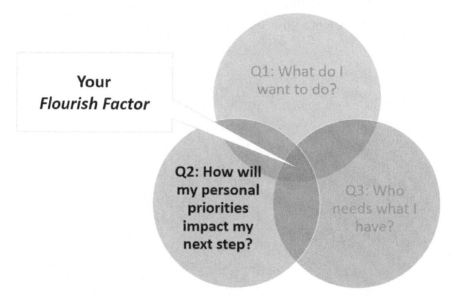

Based on where we are in our lives, at any given time, we each have personal priorities that influence our choices and our needs. These could be related to geography, financial requirements, values, organizational culture, etc.

Here are a few "real-life" examples:

– Being geographically land-locked (i.e. unable to relocate) because of kids in high school and / or aging parents

– Needing to maximize income because of life style preferences and / or changes

– Wanting to find an organizational mission that reflects personal desire to make a difference in the world

The clearer your focus around your preferences, the less time you'll waste as you explore potential options. Here's a cautionary tale:

EXAMPLE:

A marketing executive client, who lived in a rural Pennsylvania town, would have preferred to stay there, but senior leadership roles in marketing were scarce.

He was excited when he became the leading candidate with a major international spirits company. Unfortunately, placing all other opportunities on hold as he spent 8-weeks driving several hours each way to interview and demo marketing presentations — he decided to decline their generous offer when it was extended.

Why? Because at the 11th hour he said he realized he couldn't in good conscience market liquor to the world.

That should have been something he determined before derailing his transition efforts for a role that was misaligned to his personal values.

The executive had other opportunities that were aligned with his values, but they evaporated with his lack of attention to them.

The point of question #2 is to determine early in the process how your personal priorities will impact your next-best-step.

For help answering this question, work through the exercises in Chapter Three, *Career Management Diagnostic Q2: How Will My Personal Priorities Impact My Next Step?*

Question 3: Who **needs** what I have?

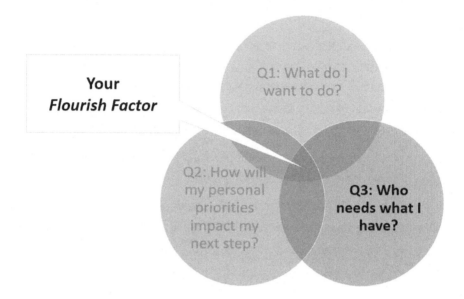

If this feels like a big question, it's because it is. The question: "Who **needs** what I have?" means:

1) What's the profile of the organization that needs my thought leadership, skills, and expertise? In other words, what organization is experiencing the problem (or pain) that I'm best at solving?

2) Who's the ultimate stakeholder for whom that issue is keeping them awake at night?

Let's pause for a moment to really dive into the 2nd part of that question. We are intentionally using the word "stakeholder" and not hiring authority or, even, decision-maker. The example on the following page will help illustrate the idea.

EXAMPLE:

An IT executive, who managed full-scale implementations of enterprise-wide IT systems for global organizations, was looking to make a change.

His focus was to work with companies (in the same industry) that were doing these large technology transformations. His value-add was his ability to accelerate new technology adoption in order to help deliver on customer commitments. Even in his IT role, he could draw the trail back to his ability to positively impact bottom-line growth.

As he began networking, he focused on CIOs, as that was the role to which he typically reported. He made great progress setting up what felt like productive networking meetings.

Unfortunately, although the CIOs all seemed receptive and promised further action, most never followed-through at all.

When we evaluated why, we were able to isolate a trend that suggested that the CIOs were threatened by his expertise and were being territorial over their domain.

Taking a step back, we determined that while the CIO was *one* of the stakeholders, they weren't the only stakeholder. The other stakeholders were the CFOs and CEOs—who might not be technologically-savvy but might have questions about making a US$65M spend on tech.

By talking with vendors in his network, he built a list of organizations that had either outstanding RFPs for new system implementations that he then cross-referenced with his network. He then targeted d the CFOs —who were slightly more accessible to him.

His networking connections facilitated introductions that sounded something like this: "I know you're getting ready to make a big spend on tech. I have a colleague who's led these kinds of tech transformations helping to speed the adoption and positively impact the bottom-line. He's offered to meet for breakfast and either help you build a list of salient questions for the Go / No Go meeting, and/or to answer any questions you might not feel comfortable asking in the presence of your team."

One of those meetings resulted in the IT Executive winning a CFO-advocate who helped him land his next-best-role.

If you need assistance identifying who needs what you have, work through the exercises in Chapter Four, *Career Management Diagnostic Q3: Who needs what I have?*

As you begin the exercises that will help you answer the 3 questions, allow us to use our extensive experience in this field to show you how clear and straight-forward the process can be. For years, we've used these exercises with our clients and have had tremendous results.

When you complete each exercise, you'll be encouraged to track results to your own *Flourish Factor* Profile. In doing so, you will create a base-line from which to compare options.

Opportunities sometimes present themselves and the profile will allow you to evaluate whether or not those opportunities are worth pursuing. In other words, you'll have a tool to help you manage your own sustainable employability.

TIP

We're often asked how this tool compares to other more formal assessments like the MBTI, DISC, Gallup StrengthsFinder, etc.

While we are certified in many of these tools and have used them in our coaching, it has been our experience that our clients were look for a clearer and more direct link between how their efforts lead to career and brand clarity.

You can easily include the results from other assessments you have taken when you're analyzing your Flourish Factor Profile.

We encourage it.

2. Career Management Diagnostic: Q1: What Do I Want to Do?

If you're starting with Question 1, then you're possibly struggling with **what you want to do** as opposed to **what you can do**. Really, it's about where you're at your best, because that is where you are the most marketable.

The exercises in this chapter are designed to help you narrow your focus, not just to inventory your skills and expertise.

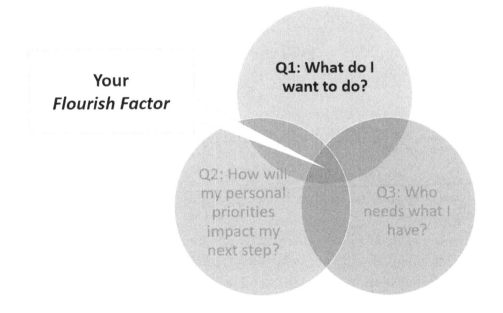

The first exercise we've included is the Marketable / Transferrable Skills Exercise, which will identify your core competencies or skill clusters. Why does that matter? Let's look at an example:

In completing the Marketable / Transferrable Skills exercise, you'll identify a laundry list of your skills – what you **can do**. But of those skills, what do you **like** to do? Of the things you **can do** and **like** to do, what are the skills at which you **excel**? That's where you're at your best and you're the most marketable. Let's illustrate what this exercise will help you accomplish.

In the diagnostic, this would generally allow you to identify 2 or 3 possible paths or viable options to consider in the context of Questions 2 and 3.

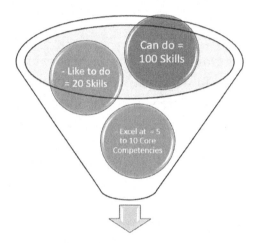

2 or 3 Viable Options or Paths

Marketable / Transferrable Skills

Regardless of the career option(s) you might be exploring, it's important to clearly identify your marketable skills, especially in the context of today's competitive job market.

This knowledge will help you identify potential audiences and present yourself well as you seek out your next-best-step. This is especially true, if you're interested in transferring your skills to other functional areas or industries.

Use the lists that follow to assist in identifying the marketable / transferrable skills you have learned or developed throughout your career.

Be sure each skill you select is supported by experience, education, or achievements.

DIRECTIONS:

1) Place a Checkmark ✓ next to all that you **can do**.

2) Next, put a line through the ✓ representing the skills you **like to do** (which will create an **X**).

3) Finally, of the skills that have an **X**, circle the ones at which you **excel**.

Administration

☐	Administrative Support	☐ Executive Support	☐	Project Management
☐	Agenda Preparation	☐ Facilitates Management	☐	Recording
☐	Assigning	☐ Filing Systems	☐	Reporting
☐	Billing Systems	☐ Following up	☐	Resource Management
☐	Board of Directors	☐ General Accounting	☐	Restructuring
☐	Budget Administration	☐ Health / Safety	☐	Sales Support
☐	Cataloging	☐ Human Resources	☐	Scheduling
☐	Categorizing	☐ Inventory Control	☐	Statutory Reporting
☐	Client Relations	☐ Legal Counsel	☐	Strategic Planning
☐	Contract Negotiations	☐ Media Relations	☐	System Administration
☐	Coordinating	☐ Meeting Minutes	☐	System Integration
☐	Correcting	☐ Office Management	☐	Training / Learning Development
☐	Corporate Records	☐ Operations	☐	Travel Arrangements
☐	Corporate Secretary	☐ Organizational Development	☐	Vendor Selection / Management
☐	Developing Timelines	☐ Planning	☐	Other:
☐	Document Management	☐ Policies / Procedures	☐	Other:
☐	Event Planning	☐ Process Improvement	☐	Other:

Client / Customer Relations

☐ Account Management	☐ Customer Surveys	☐ Problem Resolution
☐ Administration	☐ Data Management	☐ Process Improvement
☐ Brand Delivery	☐ Handling Complaints	☐ Project Management
☐ Building Loyalty	☐ Inbound Calling	☐ Promotions
☐ Building Relationships	☐ Incentive Programs	☐ Reception
☐ Call Center Management	☐ Issues Management	☐ Relationship Management
☐ Client Relations	☐ Loyalty Programs	☐ Root Cause Analysis
☐ Complaint Resolution	☐ Media Relations	☐ Sales Support
☐ Corporate Communications	☐ Networking	☐ Scheduling
☐ Customer Capture	☐ Order Processing	☐ Screening Calls
☐ Customer Loyalty	☐ Outbound Calling	☐ Service Benchmarks
☐ Customer Relations	☐ Policies + Procedures	☐ Service Contracts / SLAs
☐ Customer Retention	☐ Post-Sales Support	☐ Telemarketing
☐ Customer Satisfaction	☐ Pre-Sales Support	☐ Other:
☐ Customer Service	☐ Privacy Protection	☐ Other:

Communications

☐ Advertising	☐ Influencing	☐ Presenting Ideas
☐ Brand Management	☐ Interviewing	☐ Promotions
☐ Branding	☐ Lead Generation	☐ Proof Reading
☐ Business Development	☐ Lecturing	☐ Public Relations (PR)
☐ Client Servicing	☐ Listening	☐ Public Speaking
☐ Corporate Communication	☐ Managing Conflict	☐ Relating

☐	Corporate Sales	☐	Marketing Commu- nication (MarCom)	☐	Resolving Issues
☐	Corresponding	☐	Marketing	☐	Sales
☐	Debating	☐	Marketing Management	☐	Sales Management
☐	Defending a Client / Company	☐	Media Relations	☐	Sales Planning
☐	Defending a Position	☐	Mediating	☐	Selling
☐	Drawing	☐	Negotiating	☐	Teaching
☐	Editing	☐	Online Marketing	☐	Writing
☐	Facilitating	☐	Persuading	☐	Other:

Data Analytics

☐	Assessing Quality	☐	Evaluating	☐	Researching
☐	Benchmarking	☐	Forecasting	☐	Setting Standards
☐	Business Intelligence Reporting	☐	Gathering Data	☐	Taking Inventory
☐	Comparing	☐	Interpreting	☐	Visually Communi- cating Data
☐	Computing	☐	Managing Documents	☐	Visually Presenting Data
☐	Creating Repeatabil- ity (R, Python)	☐	Managing Information	☐	Other:
☐	Data Analysis	☐	Measuring	☐	Other:
☐	Data Modeling	☐	Observing	☐	Other:

Engineering

☐	Architectural Design	☐	Industrial Engineering	☐	Program Management
☐	Bid Proposal	☐	Justification Study	☐	Project Management
☐	Bill of Materials	☐	Just in Time	☐	Prototype Testing
☐	Capital Management	☐	Kaizen / Kanban	☐	Quality Assurance
☐	cGMP / cGDP / cGLP	☐	Lean Manufacturing	☐	Quality Engineering
☐	Code Compliance	☐	Materials Management	☐	Quality Improvement
☐	Conserving Energy	☐	Mechanical Engineering	☐	Research & Development (R&D)
☐	Commissioning	☐	New Product Launch	☐	Resource Management
☐	Continuous Improvement	☐	Plant Engineering	☐	RFP / RFQ / RFI
☐	Design Engineering	☐	PPAP / APQP	☐	Root Cause Analysis
☐	Design Specifications	☐	Process Capability Analysis	☐	Statistical Analysis
☐	Drafting	☐	Process Costing	☐	Systems Integration
☐	Engineering	☐	Process Engineering	☐	Technical Documentation
☐	Documentation	☐	Process Flow Mapping	☐	Total Quality Management
☐	Environmental Engineering	☐	Process Improvement	☐	Vendor Management
☐	Environmental Permitting	☐	Process Standardization	☐	Vibration and Drop Testing
☐	Failure Analysis	☐	Product Close-out	☐	Other:
☐	Feasibility Analysis	☐	Product Development	☐	Other:
☐	Final Customer Acceptance	☐	Product Reliability	☐	Other:
☐	Greenfield	☐	Productivity Improvement	☐	Other:

Facilities & Construction Management

☐ Architectural Design	☐ Liaison	☐ Renovating
☐ Bid Proposal	☐ Location Identification	☐ Safety
☐ Code Compliance	☐ Managing Energy Systems	☐ Scheduling
☐ Conserving Energy	☐ Managing Facilities	☐ Surveying
☐ Controlling Quality	☐ Materials Planning	☐ Toxicity Reduction
☐ Cost Estimating	☐ Optimizing Energy Use	☐ Traffic Management
☐ Designing	☐ Planning	☐ Vendor / Supplier Negotiating
☐ Drafting	☐ Preventative Maintenance	☐ Vendor / Supplier Sourcing
☐ Environmental Compliance / Restoration	☐ Project feasibility analysis	☐ Waste Reduction
☐ Ergonomics	☐ Project Management	☐ Waste Water Reduction
☐ Fault Analysis	☐ Reading Schematics	☐ Water Reclamation
☐ Forecasting	☐ Recycling / Reclaiming	☐ Other:
☐ Green Sustainability (LEEDS)	☐ Reducing	☐ Other:
☐ Integrating Technology	☐ Repairing	☐ Other:

Financial Management

☐ Accounts Payable	☐ Corporate Tax	☐ IPO
☐ Accounts Receivable	☐ Cost Accounting	☐ Letters of Credit
☐ Adjusted Present Value	☐ Cost Avoidance	☐ Liability Management
☐ Angel Investing / Financing	☐ Cost Benefit Analysis	☐ Liquidation / Bankruptcy
☐ Asset Management	☐ Credit Management	☐ Managing Contracts
☐ Asset Disposition	☐ Developing Policies	☐ Mergers and Acquisitions
☐ Asset Securitization	☐ Developing Proposals	☐ Negotiating
☐ Audit Controls	☐ Divestitures	☐ Payroll

☐	Auditing	☐	Due Diligence	☐	Private Equity
☐	Audit Preparation	☐	Earnings Per Share	☐	Procurement
☐	Balance Sheet	☐	EBITDA	☐	Reconciling
☐	Basel I, II, III	☐	Financial Modeling	☐	Reporting / Analysis
☐	Budgeting	☐	Foreign Exchange	☐	Reverse Take-Over
☐	Business Planning	☐	Forecasting	☐	ROE / ROI / ROA
☐	Business Re-engineering	☐	GAAP / GATT	☐	Sarbanes Oxley
☐	Capital Financing	☐	General Accounting	☐	Systems Migration
☐	Capital Gains / Loss	☐	General Ledger	☐	Tax Planning / Management
☐	Cash Flow / Management	☐	Growing Margins	☐	Treasury
☐	Collections	☐	Hedging	☐	Vendor Sourcing
☐	Commercial Paper	☐	IFRS	☐	Other:
☐	Controlling	☐	Internal Controls	☐	Other:
☐	Corporate Governance	☐	Investor Relations	☐	Other:

International Relations

☐	Bartering	☐	Cultural Sensitivity	☐	International Licensing
☐	Bill of Exchange / Draft	☐	Customs	☐	International Marketing
☐	Bill of Lading	☐	Diplomatic Protocol	☐	Learning Languages
☐	Channels	☐	Exporting	☐	Localization
☐	Counter Purchase Offset	☐	Foreign Exchange Management	☐	Marketing
	Counter Trade		Immigration		Other:
☐	Cross Cultural Awareness	☐	Importing	☐	Other:

Leadership

☐ Active listening	☐ Empowering Others	☐ Partnering
☐ Attracting a Following	☐ Engaging Others	☐ Providing Feedback
☐ Benchmarking	☐ Influencing	☐ Risk Taking
☐ Building a Shared Vision	☐ Leading	☐ Strategizing
☐ Coaching	☐ Making Decisions	☐ Taking Command
☐ Collaborating	☐ Mentoring	☐ Visioning
☐ Consensus Building	☐ Motivating	☐ Other:

Manufacturing & Production

☐ Code Compliance	☐ Managing Facilities	☐ Repairing
☐ Conserving Energy	☐ Managing Factories / Plants	☐ Safety
☐ Controlling Quality	☐ Planning	☐ Scheduling
☐ Cost Estimating	☐ Manufacturing	☐ Shipping & Receiving
☐ Environmental Compliance	☐ Materials Planning	☐ Sourcing
☐ Ergonomics	☐ Optimizing Energy Use	☐ Statistical Process Control
☐ Fault Analysis	☐ Planning	☐ Time & Motion Studies
☐ Forecasting	☐ Production Management	☐ Toxicity Reduction
☐ Integrating Technology	☐ Project Feasibility Analysis	☐ Vendor / Supplier Negotiating
☐ Inventory Planning	☐ Project Management	☐ Warehousing
☐ Just in Time	☐ Reading and Interpreting Blueprint / Schematics	☐ Waste Reduction
☐ Lean Manufacturing / Kaizen	☐ Recycling	☐ Workflow
☐ Liaison	☐ Reducing Waste	☐ Vendor / Supplier Sourcing
☐ Managing Energy Systems	☐ Relationship Management	☐ Other:

Operations Management

☐ Advising	☐ Facility Management	☐ Outsourcing
☐ Approving	☐ Governance	☐ Performance Management
☐ Business Planning	☐ Growing Margins	☐ Plant Operations
☐ Business Reengineering	☐ Growing Revenue	☐ Process Improvement
☐ Capacity Planning	☐ Health / Safety	☐ Process Reengineering
☐ Capital Budget	☐ Implementation Management	☐ Procurement
☐ Capital Management	☐ Internal Quality Audits	☐ Profit and Loss (P&L)
☐ Change Management	☐ Interpreting Policy	☐ Project Management
☐ Code Compliance	☐ Inventory Control	☐ Quality Control
☐ Collective Bargaining	☐ Inventory Management	☐ Resource Management
☐ Consulting	☐ ISO 9001, 9002	☐ RFP / PRQ / PRFI
☐ Continuous Improvement	☐ Just in Time (JIT)	☐ Restructuring
☐ Contract Negotiations	☐ Labor Analysis	☐ Risk Management
☐ Cost Avoidance	☐ Labor Relations	☐ Six Sigma
☐ Customer Service	☐ Managing Assets	☐ Strategic Planning
☐ Decision Making	☐ Managing People	☐ Supply Chain Management
☐ Delegating	☐ Managing Timelines	☐ Training / Learning Development
☐ Developing Procedures	☐ Mergers and Acquisitions	☐ Transportation
☐ Developing Systems	☐ Multi-Site Operations	☐ Vendor Management
☐ Directing	☐ Operating Budgets	☐ Warehouse Management
☐ Distribution Management	☐ Organizational Development	☐ Other:

Planning

☐ Analyzing	☐ Creating Timelines	☐ Time Management
☐ Arranging	☐ Event Planning	☐ Workflow Management
☐ Conceptualizing	☐ Organizing	☐ Writing
☐ Creating	☐ Strategizing	☐ Other:
☐ Creating Structure	☐ Surveying	☐ Other:

Research + Development

☐ Analyzing	☐ Data Modeling	☐ Needs Assessment
☐ Assigning	☐ Deposing	☐ Observing
☐ Budget Administration	☐ Discovering	☐ Project Management
☐ Cataloging	☐ Formulating	☐ Quality Control
☐ Categorizing	☐ Gathering Data	☐ Researching
☐ Communicating	☐ Hypothesizing	☐ Reviewing
☐ Comparing	☐ Interpreting	☐ Surveying
☐ Conceptualizing	☐ Managing Teams	☐ Validating
☐ Data Analytics	☐ Measuring	☐ Other:

Sales + Marketing

☐ Account Management	☐ Developing Channels	☐ Pricing
☐ Advertising	☐ Direct Marketing	☐ Product Design
☐ Advertising Strategy	☐ Distributor Management	☐ Product Expertise
☐ Agency Management	☐ Field Sales	☐ Product Launch
☐ Analyzing Markets	☐ Following up	☐ Product Management
☐ B2B/ B2C / B2G / B2Cy	☐ Fortune 100 / 500 Sales	☐ Product Positioning
☐ Brand Acquisition	☐ Fulfillment	☐ Profit Margin
☐ Brand Management	☐ Gatherer	☐ Promoting
☐ Branding	☐ Hunter	☐ Promotions

☐ Budget / P&L	☐ Influencing	☐ Proposal Development
☐ Building Loyalty	☐ Informing Customers	☐ Prospecting
☐ Business Development	☐ Inside Sales	☐ Public Relations
☐ Campaign Management	☐ Interactive Presentations	☐ Relationship Building
☐ Category Management	☐ Key Performance Indicators (KPIs)	☐ Reputation Management
☐ Channel Sales	☐ Launching Products	☐ Resource Management
☐ Closing	☐ Line Extension	☐ Retail Sales
☐ Cold Calling	☐ Managing Products	☐ Sales Analysis
☐ Competitive Analysis	☐ Managing Sales	☐ Sales Forecasting
☐ Consultative Sales	☐ Margin Contribution	☐ Sales Leadership
☐ Consumer Surveys	☐ Margin Improvement	☐ Sales Presentations
☐ Contacting	☐ Market Analysis	☐ Sales Solutions
☐ Contract Management	☐ Market Segmentation	☐ Social Media Marketing
☐ Contract Negotiations	☐ Marketing Collateral	☐ Strategic Marketing
☐ Copy Writing	☐ Media Buy	☐ Territory Management
☐ Creative Design	☐ Media Production	☐ Trade Marketing
☐ CRM	☐ Merchandising	☐ Trend Analysis
☐ Customer Capture	☐ Multichannel Sales	☐ Value Added Reseller
☐ Customer Loyalty	☐ Negotiating	☐ Vendor Management
☐ Customer Service	☐ Product Launches	☐ Other:
☐ Deal Structuring	☐ Presenting	☐ Other:

Supply Chain Management

☐ Asset Management	☐ Inventory Control	☐ Project Management
☐ Capital Budget	☐ ISO 9001 / 9002	☐ Resource Management
☐ Change Management	☐ Just in Time (JIT)	☐ RFP / RFQ / RFI
☐ Continuous Improvement	☐ Kanban Inventory	☐ Route Management
☐ Contract Negotiations	☐ Labor Relations	☐ Service Level Agreements (SLA)
☐ Cost Accounting	☐ Logistics / Logistics Planning	☐ Shipping & Receiving
☐ Cost Reduction	☐ Materials Planning	☐ Six Sigma
☐ Customs Compliance	☐ MRP, MRP II, ERP	☐ Strategic Planning
☐ Demand Planning	☐ Multi-Site Operations	☐ Supply Chain Management
☐ Distribution Management	☐ Ocean, Air & Land Freight	☐ Tariff Rating & Traffic
☐ Facility Management	☐ Operating Budget	☐ TQM
☐ Fleet Management	☐ Outsourcing	☐ Transportation
☐ HAZMET	☐ Performance Improvement	☐ Truck Load / LTL / Cartage
☐ Health & Safety	☐ Process Improvement	☐ Vendor Management
☐ Import / Export	☐ Procurement	☐ Warehouse Management
☐ Internal Quality Audits	☐ Profit & Loss	☐ Other:

Talent Management / Human Resources

☐ Aligning Talent	☐ Employee Surveys	☐ Orientation
☐ Annual Appraisals	☐ Executive Search	☐ Pay for Performance
☐ Assessment	☐ Facilitation	☐ Pension Administration
☐ Assessment + Selection	☐ Grievances	☐ Performance Management
☐ Behavioral Interviewing	☐ Health and Safety Programs	☐ Professional Development
☐ Benchmarking	☐ Hiring	☐ Program Design
☐ Benefit Administration	☐ HR Policies / Procedures	☐ Program Management
☐ Business Reengineering	☐ HRIS / Technology	☐ Providing Feedback
☐ Certifying Professionals	☐ Human Capital Management	☐ Recruiting
☐ Change Management	☐ Instructional Design	☐ Regulatory Affairs
☐ Coaching	☐ Interviewing	☐ Rewards + Recognition
☐ Collective Bargaining	☐ Investigating	☐ Salary Reviews
☐ Compensation	☐ Job Analyses	☐ Staffing
☐ Contract Negotiations	☐ Job Descriptions	☐ Strategic HR Planning
☐ Culture Management	☐ Labor Relations	☐ Succession Planning
☐ Designing Systems	☐ Leadership Development	☐ Talent Management
☐ Developing Policies	☐ Learning and Development	☐ Team Building
☐ Diversity Management	☐ Managing Change	☐ Training
☐ Employee Engagement	☐ Mentoring	☐ Vendor Management
☐ Employee Experience	☐ Mentoring	☐ Workforce Planning
☐ Employee Handbook	☐ Onboarding / Assimilation	☐ Other:
☐ Employee Relations	☐ Organizational Development	☐ Other:
☐ Employee Retention	☐ Organizational Effectiveness	☐ Other:

Technical / Systems Management

☐ Administration	☐ IaaS	☐ Root Cause Analysis
☐ API	☐ Imaging	☐ SaaS
☐ Application Technology	☐ Information / Cyber Security	☐ Scientific Research
☐ Applications:	☐ Infrastructure Development	☐ SDLC
☐ Artificial Intelligence	☐ Installing	☐ Security
☐ BSS / OSS	☐ Inventing	☐ Server Management
☐ Business Continuity	☐ LAN / WAN	☐ Site Assessment
☐ Business Transformation	☐ Languages:	☐ Software Configuration
☐ Capital Budgets	☐ Legacy Systems	☐ Solutions Delivery
☐ Change Management	☐ Licensing	☐ Storing
☐ Classifying	☐ MIS	☐ Systems Administration (SysAdmin)
☐ Cloud	☐ Monitoring	☐ Systems Analysis
☐ Coding	☐ Multiplatform Integration	☐ Systems Configuration
☐ Computing	☐ Network Administration	☐ Systems Deployment
☐ Cross-Development Tools:	☐ Operating Systems:	☐ Systems Development
☐ Data Analysis	☐ PaaS	☐ Systems Management
☐ Data Architecture	☐ Performing Maintenance	☐ Technical Documentation
☐ Data Center Operations	☐ Platforms:	☐ Technical Writing
☐ Data Gathering	☐ Process Reengineering	☐ Tooling
☐ Data Recovering	☐ Processors:	☐ Training
☐ Database Administration	☐ Product Launch	☐ Troubleshooting
☐ Database Development	☐ Product Testing	☐ Vendor Management
☐ Database Management	☐ Programming	☐ Virtual Reality
☐ Debugging	☐ Project Management	☐ VoIP
☐ Designing	☐ Protocols:	☐ Web Design
☐ Developing Products	☐ Quality Assurance	☐ Web Master
☐ Disaster Recovery	☐ Query Development	☐ Web-based Technology
☐ Embedded Systems	☐ Interpreting Blueprint / Schematics	☐ Wiring / Rewiring

☐	End User Support	☐	Reliability Testing	☐	Workflow Management
☐	Engineering	☐	Repairing	☐	Yield Management
☐	Enterprise Architecture	☐	Report Writing	☐	Other:
☐	Equipment:	☐	Requirements Gathering	☐	Other:
☐	Fault Analysis	☐	Research and Development	☐	Other:
☐	GIS	☐	Resource Management	☐	Other:

List 10 or more of your top marketable / transferrable skills below.

Next, look for patterns where your top skills are clustered together as that represents your primary functional areas of expertise (or core competencies), such as Communications or Operations Management. This is important because it will ultimately help you narrow down your viable options or possible paths.

List the primary functional areas of expertise identified above.

Identify your top 6 skills from within those primary functional areas of expertise and track your results to your *Flourish Factor* Profile found in Chapter Five. In addition, be sure to track your top 3 functional areas of expertise as they represent where you're most likely to flourish.

See the APPENDIX for additional exercises on this topic.

Irrepressible Skills

When you are successful, it is usually because you are applying your skills and strengths, and because your personal traits are assets for the task-at-hand.

A key element of this analysis is the identification of **recurring patterns or themes**. These skills are what we call Irrepressible Skills.

Irrepressible Skills are really your strengths and represent your sweet spot. They are likely the things you do so naturally and instinctively that you may or may not even be aware of them.

As noted strengths expert Marcus Buckingham has said: "They are the things you do that make you strong." When you do them, you're so engaged in what you're doing that you lose track of time. (For more on strengths, see the APPENDIX.)

Therefore, an analysis of your achievements, accomplishments, and successes can lead to a clear definition of these skills and traits.

The formula by which to write about these experiences is to tell a story in the format of S-T-A-R-S.

The S T-A-R-S formula means:

S – Scope: Describe the scope or problem with which you or your teams were faced.

T – Task: Describe the specific tasks and why they were such a challenge or so important.

A – Action: Describe what you did (i.e. your actions). Start your actions with an action verb. (See the APPENDIX for a list of Action Verbs.)

R – Result: Describe how the company, client, or customer benefited from the action(s) you or your team took.

S – Significance: Why did it matter?

Note: There will be more on this later in Chapter Six.

TIP

How do you come up with the content about which to write S-T-A-R-S Stories?

Brainstorm a list of experiences you've had. Start with skills, knowledge, or expertise that employers are seeking, and then filter to pick the best examples (those you'd want to share with an employer or networking contact) and write them out.

Here's a list of ideas from which to generate your stories:

1) In-Demand Skills exercise

2) Marketable / Transferrable Skills exercise

3) Anything of which you're proud in your life (professional and personal)

4) Awards or Accolades (sometimes others appreciate what we do more than we do)

5) Performance Appraisals / Reviews (what you did well in any given year)

6) Old Résumé / CVs (to remind you of work experiences)

7) Old Position Descriptions (to remind you of work experiences)

8) Work Samples (things you may have written, created, or developed)

To further help, check out the APPENDIX for a list of Action Verbs that might also help you craft the stories.

Ideas for Results

Per the tip on the previous page, it's important that when writing your S-T-A-R-S stories that you clearly articulate the benefit or result your efforts generated.

Here is a list of sample phrases that may help you more clearly spell out those benefits. Remember the rule of thumb -- if you can't quantify, then "qualify" your results.

Make money	
Grew Revenue Streams	Generated Profits
Improved Image (e.g. Corporate)	Increased Awareness
Expanded Product Line	Shortened Lead Time
Increased Sales	Developed New Products
Identified Adjacent Revenue Streams	Increased Customer Satisfaction
Increased Inventory Turns	Built/Increased Brand Awareness
Innovated New Products/Ideas	Increased Earnings
Increased Return on Investment	Reduced Capital Investment

Save money	
Reduced Turnover	Minimized Risk and / or Liability
Improved Accuracy	Reduced A/R Days Out
Reduced Rejects	Improved Methods & Processes
Upgraded Plans	Designed Equipment
Ensured Safety	Reduced Energy Requirements
Improved Customer Relations	Enhanced Operations
Reduced Errors	Improved Morale
Reduced Costs	Drove Quality Improvements

Save time (because Time = Money)	
Automated Systems	Upgraded Training
Reduced Downtime	Increased Productivity
Enhanced Efficiencies	Streamlined Procedures
Improved Performance	Eliminated Unnecessary Processes

S-T-A-R-S Stories

Irrepressible Skill #1:

Choose a work-related accomplishment from your recent history. Be as specific and relevant as you can, selecting an experience within the past 12-months.

Describe the scope or
problem
S (Scope)

Explain the task ... what was
your challenge and / or why it
was so important

T (Task)

List the specific actions to
show you how you resolved
the problem

A (Action)

What was the result or
accomplishment and what
were the benefits? Can the
result be quantified or
qualified?

R (Result)

Why did it matter? What skills
were you using? What traits
and strengths did you
employ?

S (Significance)

Irrepressible Skill #2:

Choose a work-related accomplishment an experience within a 3-year window.

Describe the scope or
problem

S (Scope)

Explain the task ... what was
your challenge and / or why it
was so important

T (Task)

List the specific actions to
show you how you resolved
the problem

A (Action)

What was the result or
accomplishment and what
were the benefits? Can the
result be quantified or
qualified?

R (Result)

Why did it matter? What skills
were you using? What traits
and strengths did you
employ?

S (Significance)

Irrepressible Skill #3:

Choose a work-related accomplishment an experience from 7-year window.

Describe the scope or
problem

S (Scope)

Explain the task ... what was
your challenge and / or why it
was so important

T (Task)

List the specific actions to
show you how you resolved
the problem

A (Action)

What was the result or
accomplishment and what
were the benefits? Can the
result be quantified or
qualified?

R (Result)

Why did it matter? What skills
were you using? What traits
and strengths did you
employ?

S (Significance)

Irrepressible Skill #4:

Choose a work-related accomplishment an experience from within a 10- to 15-year window.

Describe the scope or
problem

S (Scope)

Explain the task ... what was
your challenge and / or why it
was so important

T (Task)

List the specific actions to
show you how you resolved
the problem

A (Action)

What was the result or
accomplishment and what
were the benefits? Can the
result be quantified or
qualified?

R (Result)

Why did it matter? What skills
were you using? What traits
and strengths did you
employ?

S (Significance)

Irrepressible Skill #5:

Choose a work-related accomplishment an experience during anytime in your entire career.

Describe the scope or
problem

S (Scope)

Explain the task ... what was
your challenge and / or why it
was so important

T (Task)

List the specific actions to
show you how you resolved
the problem

A (Action)

What was the result or
accomplishment and what
were the benefits? Can the
result be quantified or
qualified?

R (Result)

Why did it matter? What skills
were you using? What traits
and strengths did you
employ?

S (Significance)

Irrepressible Skill #6:

Choose a personal accomplishment -- volunteer, hobby, college, etc.

Describe the scope or
problem

S (Scope)

Explain the task ... what was
your challenge and / or why it
was so important

T (Task)

List the specific actions to
show you how you resolved
the problem

A (Action)

What was the result or
accomplishment and what
were the benefits? Can the
result be quantified or
qualified?

R (Result)

Why did it matter? What skills
were you using? What traits
and strengths did you
employ?

S (Significance)

Note any patterns or repeats and transfer them to the *Flourish Factor* Profile in
Chapter Five.

3. Career Management Diagnostic Q2: How Will My Personal Priorities Impact My Next Step?

With Question 2, our goal is help you gain clarity around the factors in your current situation which will drive your decision-making process – as understanding your priorities will help you better focus your time and efforts.

Life Vision

A professional objective is easier to set when you have a clear idea of your destination. In other words, where do you want to be when you're done?

So rather than consider specific career goals, we'd like you to think about a Life Vision. Consider the following questions, issues, or factors.

– When you look at your life as-a-whole, where do you want to be next year? In 3-years? 5-years from now?

- How old will you be? How old will your children be?
- Where will you be living?
- To what age will you work?
- Will you work full-time? Part-time?
- Will you have just one job or several ways of bringing in revenue (participating in the gig- or on-demand economy)?
- What do you want to be doing?
- Is there a specific job to which you aspire?
- Is there a specific expertise you would like to use?
- Are you working for a company or for yourself?

You get the idea. List below what you want your LIFE to look like. If you don't have a clear picture, then simply list what you can – to the best of your ability.

TIP

Keep in mind, the vision you manifest for the next 1- to 3-years may not be the same as what you would envision for yourself in 5– or 10-years.

In other words, the circumstances of our lives greatly affect our ideal vision.

This relates directly back to Question #2: How will my personal priorities impact my next step?

EXAMPLE:

The client who decided he wanted to be a CFO in 5 years, yet was missing both an MBA and Treasury experience.

By having a clear picture of where he wanted to end up, he was able to build a plan to fill the gaps.

He pursued an internal opportunity (a lateral move), that gave him the Treasury experience and worked on his MBA after hours. This positioned him well as a CFO-candidate.

You'll revisit this exercise once you're finalizing your focus.

Environmental *Flourish Factors*

As we've discussed, there are environments where you'll do fine and others in which you'll flourish: feeling that you're giving the best of what you have to offer, that it's appreciated, valued, and that you're getting to be your best-self-at-work every day. We call these Environmental Flourish Factors.

DIRECTIONS: This exercise has 2-steps:

1) Review the following list of Environmental Flourish Factors and categorize each of them into the table in Chapter Five.

2) Prioritize the results.

Environment *Flourish Factors*

1)	Achievement-Oriented Environment	Work where there is a sense of accomplishment; being able to see results generated from the tasks I undertake, challenges I overcome, or assignments I complete.
2)	Alignment with Boss	Work with a boss with whom I have a positive relationship, either as a supervisor, mentor, or someone who shares my values and vision.
3)	Autonomy / Independence	Work in an environment where my work is self-directed, where I'm given the objectives and the latitude to make it happen within deadlines, but in my own way or within my own organizational style.

4)	Commute	Work is within what I consider to be a reasonable range of home so that commuting distance isn't detracting from quality-of-life.
5)	Competition	Work that allows me to pit my abilities against others and where there are clear win-and-lose outcomes.
6)	Contact with Others	Work in an environment where I have extensive day-to-day interactions with others, inside or outside the organization.
7)	Controlled Chaos	Work in either a loosely-defined or an undefined environment, where priorities may often be unclear, perhaps in a start-up or entrepreneurial environment, or a place where the rules are made up as you go along.
8)	Creativity / Innovation	Work in an environment that values and appreciates the generation of new ideas, programs, services, or systems; appropriately challenging the status-quo.
9)	Decision Making	Work in an environment that allows me the appropriate authority to make and act upon decisions about my assigned areas of responsibility.
10)	Diversity Friendly	Work in an environment that values and respects people from a broad range of ages, cultures, lifestyles, and/or ethnic backgrounds.
11)	Employee Benefits	Work in an environment that offers a comprehensive benefits package that meets my needs so those issues are not a distraction in my day-to-day life.
12)	Expert Status	Work in an environment that recognizes and values my expertise whether technical, functional, or skill related.
13)	Fast Pace	Work in an environment that has a high-level of energy, excitement, and activity.
14)	Financial Gain	Work in an environment where the focus is on generating high profits that will benefit the stakeholders.
15)	Friendships	Work in a culture that allows and values the formation of close personal relationships with colleagues
16)	Global Focus	Work in an organization that will potentially accommodate my desire to live and work outside my current location.
17)	Influence Others	Work in an environment that allows me to lead and influence others.
18)	Learning Environment	Work in an environment that values and supports learning, research, the pursuit of new knowledge, and/or professional development.
19)	Leave a Legacy	Work in an environment that will allow me to lead or be a part of an effort that will leave a legacy in this world, or to be the pioneer after whom others will follow.
20)	Loyalty	Work in an environment that exhibits a high level of allegiance between the organization and the employees.

21)	Moral Affiliation / Fulfillment	Work in an environment where both the organization and employees embody morals, values, and ethics that are similar to my own.
22)	Physical Challenge	Work in an environment that allows me to be physically active, not sedentary behind a desk.
23)	Physical Work Environment	Work in a setting that is physically appealing and/or environmentally conducive to help me do my best work.
24)	Prestige & Recognition	Work in an environment where I am either highly visible, well known, front and center, or the recipient of recognition by colleagues and/or customers.
25)	Professional Affiliation	Work in an organization with which I'm proud to be associated and to tell others I work there.
26)	Pure Challenge	Work in an environment that offers the chance to take on and overcome impossible obstacles, difficult problems, or tough opponents
27)	Quality-focused	Work in an environment that sets high standards, demands quality, strives for excellence, and has a low tolerance for error
28)	Risk	Work in an environment where the stakes of success or failure are high.
29)	Sky's the Limit	Work in an environment that encourages all groups (i.e. not just those at executive levels) to participate meaningfully at the highest levels of the organization.
30)	Solitude	Work in an environment where I have minimal day-to-day interactions with others, having time to work independently.
31)	Stable / Low Stress Workplace	Work in an environment with a predictable workload, manageable deadlines, with a strong element of routine, unlikely to change significantly over time.
32)	Supervision / Management	Work in a role that allows me to directly plan and manage the work/schedule of others.
33)	Teamwork	Work in an environment that allows me to collaborate with others, capitalizing on the expertise of others to reach stated objectives.
34)	Travel	Work in a role that requires me to travel a significant amount of time.
35)	Variety and Challenge	Work in an environment that is varied and dynamic, allowing me to be challenged as a professional, able to demonstrate my professional agility and adaptability.
36)	Work with Tight Deadlines	Work in an environment driven by tight timelines and critical deadlines.

EXAMPLE:

We've been ask why we call these **Environmental** *Flourish Factors* when many could be considered values.

There is strong overlap with many of these concepts and personal values. But our intention is to directly apply these concepts to your FOCUS on your next-best-step.

Recently, a Learning + Development Executive turned down what, on paper, appeared to be a dream role because one of her top 2 factors was "Contact with Others" and this role was remote — where she'd largely be working alone all day.

Must Haves (Want)	Neutral (Might Want)	Deal Breakers (Don't Want)

At this point, our concern is not with the "Might Want" column. By specifically addressing the "Must Haves" and "Deal Breakers," you're identifying the factors that you 'must have' in order to get to a yes. The 'deal breakers' are things that would cause you to walk-away from an opportunity.

However, if you're looking for something different to consider, the "Might Want" column would be a good list to explore.

Transfer your top 3 "Must Haves" and top 3 "Deal Breakers" from the table above to the *Flourish Factor* Profile found in Chapter Five.

TIP

To take this exercise 1-step further, review the list and prioritize your top 3 MUST HAVE Environmental **Flourish Factors** *and record them here along with the effect you would expect them to have on your work experience.*

My #1 Factor:

Effect on my work?

My #2 Factor:

Effect on my work?

My #3 Factor:

Effect on my work?

EXAMPLE

Factor: *Pure Challenge*

Effect on my work? *Having a new challenge keeps me interested and exciting about my job; alleviates boredom and the desire to move on every few years. A role with a focus on projects would help me challenged.*

Characteristics and Traits

Each of us possesses certain personal characteristics or traits that make us unique and enhance our ability to perform certain tasks successfully.

Let's face it, if what comes naturally to you is neither needed nor appreciated in your work or work environment, it will be difficult to be your best-self.

These characteristics determine the unique value we bring to the role we fulfill. Review the list below and put a check next to any trait that describes you best in a professional context. Be sure that there is clear evidence of your accomplishments for the traits you check.

DIRECTIONS: Check all those that apply to you and then go back and circle those that are your strongest and / or those you most value in yourself.

Characteristics and Traits

☐ Accountable	☐ Empathetic	☐ Productive
☐ Accurate	☐ Energetic	☐ Quality driven
☐ Adaptable	☐ Entertaining	☐ Quick thinker
☐ Agile	☐ Enthusiastic	☐ Rational
☐ Adventurous	☐ Future-oriented	☐ Relevant
☐ Ambitious	☐ Good attitude	☐ Resourceful
☐ Analytical	☐ Hard worker	☐ Responsible
☐ Artistic	☐ High impact	☐ Respectful
☐ Assertive	☐ High standards	☐ Responsive
☐ Big picture focused	☐ Imaginative	☐ Self-assured
☐ Bottom-line focused	☐ Independent	☐ Self-controlled
☐ Challenge driven	☐ Inquisitive	☐ Self-directed
☐ Civic-minded	☐ Intelligent	☐ Self-starter
☐ Committed	☐ Intuitive	☐ Sense of humor
☐ Communicator	☐ Kind	☐ Sensitive
☐ Compassionate	☐ Leader	☐ Sociable
☐ Conscientious	☐ Levelheaded	☐ Stable
☐ Confident	☐ Logical	☐ Story Teller

☐	Creative	☐	Loyal	☐	Tech-Savvy
☐	Cutting-edge	☐	Original	☐	Thorough
☐	Deadline driven	☐	Organized	☐	Tolerant
☐	Decisive	☐	People-oriented	☐	Trustworthy
☐	Dedicated	☐	Perfectionist	☐	Versatile
☐	Delegator	☐	Personable	☐	Visionary
☐	Dependable	☐	Persuasive	☐	Other:
☐	Design-oriented	☐	Positive	☐	Other:
☐	Discrete	☐	Practical	☐	Other:

What Are Your Workplace Priorities?

When considering your personal priorities, it's important to have a holistic perspective of what you need and / or want from your next role.

The following exercise will prompt you to dig into a deeper level of granularity when considering those priorities.

In consideration of efficiencies, this is also information that could be used later to evaluate and negotiate opportunities.

DIRECTIONS:

1) Place a Checkmark ✓ next to all items that you would consider **Nice-to-Have.**

2) Next, put a line through the ✓ (creating an **X**) identifying the items that you would you consider **Must-Haves**.

Transfer the most critical "Must-Haves" and "Nice-to-Haves" you have identified from the table to the *Flourish Factor* Profile found in Chapter Five.

What are Your Workplace Priorities?

Company Focus		Focus of Position		Compensation	
☐	Company Size	☐	Matches Brand / Focus	☐	Base Salary
☐	Sales Volume	☐	Duties / Responsibilities	☐	Bonus (Guaranteed / Potential)
☐	Number of Employees	☐	Authority	☐	Incentive
☐	Public / Private	☐	Independence	☐	Profit sharing
☐	Profit / Non-Profit	☐	Challenge	☐	Performance Evaluations
☐	National / Global Footprint	☐	High Risk / Low Risk	☐	Deferred Compensation
☐	Academic	☐	Job Visibility	☐	Sign-on Bonus
☐	Product / Service	☐	Reporting Relationships	☐	Healthcare Benefits
☐	Centralized / Decentralized	☐	Direct Line Reporting	☐	Vision / Dental / HSA
☐	Division / Subdivision	☐	Dotted Line Reporting	☐	Insurance (Disability STD / LTD / AD&D)
☐	Management Depth	☐	Level of Travel	☐	D&O Insurance
☐	Financial Condition	☐	Travel Status	☐	Retirement / Pension Plan
☐	Political Climate	☐	Title Status	☐	Car / Car Allowance
☐	Company Growth History	☐	Other:	☐	Parking
☐	Growth Trajectory / Future Growth	☐	Other:	☐	Club Membership
☐	Profitability	☐	Other:	☐	Credit Card(s)
☐	Turnaround Options	☐	Other:	☐	Financial Planning
☐	Stability	☐		☐	Tax Assistance
☐	Vulnerability to Acquisition	☐		☐	Expense Account
☐	Reputation / Brand	☐		☐	Professional Dues
☐	Market Dependency	☐		☐	Technology / Tools
☐	Other:	☐		☐	Tuition Assistance
☐	Other:	☐		☐	Other:

4. Career Management Diagnostic Q3: Who needs what I have?

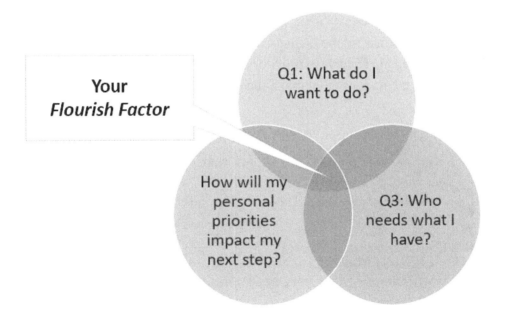

Question #3: Who needs what I have? What's the profile of the organization and who is the ultimate stakeholder who's kept awake at night by the issue for which you add the most value? As author and Forbes contributor, George Bradt, is fond of saying when he talks about employer requests in interviews, "No one cares about you. All anyone cares about is what you're going to do for them."

Remember, you're working to create a *Flourish Factor* Profile which is the confluence of each of the 3 questions. The diagnostic is intended to simply help you determine what you know versus what you don't know. As you explore who needs what you have, let's do a reality-check.

If you're a banking manager, something to consider is: Are you a manager who happens to work in banking? Or, are you a banking professional who happens to be a manager?

Keep in mind, you're essentially exploring career options. There are 4 possible dimensions:

1) Current Profession / Current Industry

> Staying in your current profession and current industry might be your simplest option. For example, if you're a Human Resources Professional who has spent your entire career in healthcare and your top priorities are to get back to work as quickly as possible while maximizing your income, then the most likely option would be to pursue current profession / current industry.

Note, if your response is: "Great, I'll stay in a similar role in the same industry." Your work still isn't done. This is the reason the *Flourish Factor* matters. It's the key ingredients in identifying work that will allow to you be your best-self-at-work. It's the nuances that make the difference.

EXAMPLE:

A client was a well-compensated Executive Assistant for a C-suite officer. She insisted she only needed "to find another job." After reviewing her *Flourish Factor* profile, however, it wasn't just another job she needed.

She realized she wanted another role where she was the executive's trusted confidante; entrusted to draft correspondence and make decisions about scheduling and appearances. She wasn't open to simply answering the phone and running personal errands such as picking up the dry cleaning.

The nuances matter.

---

2) Different Profession / Current Industry

> Changing your current profession, but staying in your current industry is a fairly common exchange. For instance, many people who have been working for the same company for many years may do this without even realizing it. Promotions often move us from one profession or function to

another; for example, consider the sales representative who is promoted to a manager. Same industry, but two separate areas of expertise (or professions).

3) Current Profession / Different Industry

Staying with your current profession, but moving to a different industry is another option.

The tasks for someone working in HR may be the same if they are in manufacturing or if they're in retail, but the environments certainly are not the same. It *feels* different to work in manufacturing than it does in retail.

The industry (as well as organizational structure) may also impact the tasks of the job. For example, one may be more dispersed, involving more travel where another may be more centralized. This relates directly to your priorities.

4) Different Profession / Different Industry

The final option, changing both your profession and industry, is the one that will require the greatest amount of research and planning.

When you change the profession as well as the industry, it will be important to have a good understanding of market trends along with a thorough understanding of the skills that are in-demand for that profession within that industry.

EXAMPLE:

The executive in banking found himself laid-off from work after 15-years. While working to identify his *Flourish Factor*, he came to the realization that he needed to return to his original career path — medicine. So, following deeper research and reflection, he found himself returning to medical school while in his mid-40s!

Identifying In-Demand Skills

Skill /skil/

Is defined as the ability to do something well; expertise. Synonyms: expertise, skillfulness, mastery, facility, ability, capability, capacity, talent, genius, adeptness, aptitude, deftness, competence, accomplishment, proficiency, know-how

Source: Dictionary.com

As great as it is to know what you ideally want to do, that can't happen in a vacuum. You need to build a composite profile of the skills that are in-demand in the marketplace. Taking into account the 4-options we discussed earlier, this is your reality-check.

This is the work you're doing to answer the "Who needs what I have?" question. The more clearly you can identify your audience, the easier it is to develop a message to hook them into wanting a conversation with you.

EXAMPLE:

If you decided as part of (Question #1: What do I want to do?) that you are, in your heart of hearts, *Cinnamon* **Rice Chex Cereal.**

But, when you do this step, you discover the demand in your market is too small to help you realistically address your personal priorities (i.e. Question #2: How will my personal priorities impact my next step?).

In that case, you have a decision to make, do you want to stay in that narrowly defined niche where it may take longer to find your next step? Or, do you want to expand your approach and position yourself more broadly as Rice Chex Cereal, because there is a bigger demand for that.

In identifying In-Demand Skills, leverage technology to help identify the most in-demand skills.

DIRECTIONS:

1) Begin by identifying at least *3 ideal job postings* considering the profession and the industry you are targeting without considering geography. This is a

research exercise and current openings in your specific market may not yield the quality of data you need to complete it.

2) Sources to use include job boards (e.g. Indeed, LinkedIn, etc.), niche industry job boards or online communities, company websites, and networking.

3) Remove headers and company information from the job descriptions. This step is important as you're trying to identify the most commonly cited skills and experience, not the company.

4) Paste the collective job descriptions into a word cloud site such as www.wordsift.org and www.tagcrowd.com.

5) Notice that you can see the most frequently used keywords in context using this tool.

6) Identify the top 10 most repeated keywords in the word cloud. Again, make sure you're focusing on functional areas of expertise and skills, not adjectives or characteristics.

TIP

How do you know it's an ideal job posting? Although not scientific, here is a "good rule of thumb."

Consider color coding the requirements, such as:

GREEN - I've got the skill and can do what they need
YELLOW - I've got the skill but perhaps it's rusty or not used in the same environment / function
RED - I don't have the skill or maybe I don't even know what it is

Now evaluate how much green is on the page versus how much red?

If the majority of the posting isn't green, it's not likely an ideal posting.

Analyzing In-Demand Skills

DIRECTIONS:

1) Apply the data from the *ideal job descriptions* portion of this exercise, and using a table, like the one that follows, list out the requirements from each posting -- side-by-side.

2) Examine what knowledge, skills, expertise, and credentials the job market is seeking in roles you would define as ideal. Target the following information:

Job Titles - what is the market calling the role you're targeting?
For instance, if your last job title was "Director of Purchasing," but all the postings you've listed are calling it "Director of Procurement" OR "Director of Global Strategic Sourcing" (which is purchasing), what does that tell you?

Spoiler alert: you need to use the new industry language or risk being perceived by your audience as someone who is out of touch.

Requirements* - what knowledge, skills, abilities, expertise, and credentials are employers seeking in their ideal candidates?

When listing out the job postings side-by-side, are there patterns in what they're seeking? For example, if you're a Project Manager, is your research showing that the majority of postings require a PMP certification?

* As a word of caution, you might see language that reflects characteristics or traits, such as team player, organized, etc. Although they're important, they're not relevant in this exercise.

In what sequence are the primary requirements ordered? Sequence matters. The requirements that are consistently listed at the top of postings generally represent those that are most in-demand. This is your reality-check as you compare yourself to the actual needs of the marketplace.

Analyzing In-Demand Skills

	Ideal Posting #1	Ideal Posting #2	Ideal Posting #3
1) Title			
2) List Knowledge			
3) Skills / Expertise			
4) Requirements			
5) Credentials			

Another option for tracking this data is to build a simple spreadsheet.

List the top 10 to 12 In-Demand Skills you have identified below:

Now that you've identified the In-Demand Skills, which do you possess? From your results, select the strongest of your In-Demand Skills to your *Flourish Factor* Profile in Chapter Five.

5. *Flourish Factor* Profile

As you've walked through each exercise so far, you've been instructed to carry some information here to the *Flourish Factor* Profile.

What you have created, if you did that, is an excellent tool for identifying your sweet spot, that is, the profile of where you *flourish*.

It represents the key ingredients in identifying roles and environments that will allow to you be your best-self-at-work.

The closer you get to matching this profile, the better the fit. In other words, this an **evaluation tool** against which to compare your top 2 or 3 viable options.

Let's dive in.

TIP - WHY YOUR *FLOURISH FACTOR* MATTERS

Targeting a role that is within your sweet spot creates great balance in the employment equation.

You want a role that allows you to give the best of what you have to offer, and that's exactly the kind of candidate an employer wants to hire.

Consistently, we hear from employers and executive recruiters that they're seeking candidates who are clear about their ideal role. Because, that's where the candidate will be at their best!

Employers want to hire a candidate who's interests and strengths match their needs -- that candidate — if hired — is more likely to be fully engaged, productive, and more likely to stick around longer.

In this way, the employer gets more for their money.

Review the In-Demand skills along with your Marketable / Transferrable Skills that you previously completed. How do your skills, experience, and your credentials compare? Where's the overlap? Do they suggest a viable option, possible path, or target?

Are there gaps in what the market is demanding relative to your skills, experience, and credentials? How can you close those gaps? And, do you want to close those gaps?

Marketable / Transferrable Skills

Functional Areas of Expertise

Irrepressible Skills - Patterns

In-Demand Skills

Knowing who you are is important as you're looking to focus on your best-next-step. However, that has to be considered in context of the environment.

When considering your traits, it's important to realize that they're part of who you are; what makes you unique. When you're working in a job / an environment where those traits are needed and / or appreciated, it becomes easier to be your best-self-at-work.

For instance, we had a client who, the minute she identified her top traits, immediately realized why she'd not been happy in her previous job. Her traits where neither needed in the role nor were they appreciated.

Characteristics / Traits

If you're clear about your **top 2 or 3 viable options**, then consider:

1) How do they compare to your **Environmental Flourish Factors?**

Must-Haves (Want)   **Deal Breakers (Don't Want)**

2) How to do they compare to what you articulated when you completed the **Life Vision Exercise**?

If you're not yet clear about your **top 2 or 3 viable options**, complete the **Be a Better Storyteller exercise** (Chapter Six) which can help you gain focus and provide language for your messaging.

6. Be a Better Storyteller

The reality in today's job market is that you need to be able to describe **who you are in terms of where you add value** –you have to be a storyteller.

As Kristie Hedges, author of *Executive Presence* says, "Stories grab us ... shared stories accelerate interpersonal connection. Learning to tell stories to capture, direct and sustain the attention of others is a key leadership skill."

She goes on to talk about how important it is to write down your stories, using a strong structure, and having clarity about important points.

You began this process with the Irrepressible Skills exercise (Chapter Two) and we're now going to take this exercise to the next level.

Our goal is to ***make you a 'better storyteller.'***

TIP

This exercise and the Irrepressible Skills exercise are based on a commonly used model for answering Behavior Based Interviewing questions (from DDI, Inc.).

At this point, Behavior Based Interviewing is the most common type of interview.

Research from the world's leading career management companies show that more than 75% of all interviews today are Behavior Based. That means, if you're going to be prepared for interviews, you'll need these stories.

This exercise will help with two important things. First, it will help determine your FOCUS by identifying patterns of where you're at your best. Secondly, painting a picture of the audience who most needs and would want what you have to offer.

The truth is, when reflecting on experiences, we often focus on the details of the experiences rather than the patterns. To make an analogy, it's like describing the wheat stalk from the perspective of standing in the middle of the field.

You need to step back to get a broader focal point. Our goal is to help you describe the patterns in the **crop circles**, which you can't do when you're standing in the middle of the wheat field.

The point is to identify **patterns** in your experience by capturing them in writing so you have data to analyze.

To stick with the analogy, identifying those patterns will help you better manage how you farm.

If you completed the Irrepressible Skills exercise, you were asked to write out stories from specific times in your life. Now we're going to expand on that exercise.

Note: If you've not yet completed that Irrepressible Skills exercise in Chapter Two, you'll need to do that now.

TIP

Once, we worked with 2 sales executives with similar backgrounds (level, industry, size organization, etc.) who both reported they wanted to develop people in their next role.

And they were both right. Not only was it a strength for each of them, but for each of them, it was their particular sweet spot.

However, when the clients went through the exercises that follow, they each reached different conclusions.

One reported that he wanted to train the new sales force of an organization, because that would create the foundation going forward for the company.

The other reported that he wanted to take folks who were already pretty good at their jobs and develop them into super-stars and get them promoted.

*Each is an example of developing people, but are **differently nuanced**.*

If either of them found themselves in a role that was like the other wanted, they could certainly do it and probably be successful at it. But they wouldn't be as satisfied as they would be if they were in the role they identified that would play to their strengths.

Identifying Patterns in your Irrepressible Skills Stories

Once you have your stories in writing, step out of the wheat field, and review them objectively – what are the **crop circles**.

As we've said, this process is designed to help you identify where you're at your best and to start to paint a picture of the audience who needs and wants what you offer.

One of the simplest ways to accomplish that is to look at your history. Where do you thrive or lose yourself in your efforts? In other words, on what activities do you look up and realize that hours have passed and you've not noticed?

Through the next part of this exercise, our goal is to give you a broader focal point and help you identify those patterns. It's important to complete these next steps as thoroughly as you can.

Step One

Looking at the stories you've created, organize them in order of your preference (starting with #1, 2, and so forth). Even if you liked all the experiences, the first story should be your favorite or the one you'd **replicate** given the chance.

The last stories on your list might represent those experiences that although you may have enjoyed them when you did them, your instincts either say "I've **been there, done that**" or they were great, but not as good as the other experiences.

Once you have ranked your stories, note any similarities in the top 3 stories; the same with the final 3 stories. As another option, consider contrasting them.

What patterns exist in terms of similarities? Contrast?

Step Two

Relative to the Career Management Diagnostic, ask yourself the following questions looking for patterns where applicable. Note, sometimes your answers will have significance, other times they won't.

Related to Question #1: What do I WANT to do, because where you're at your best is where you are most marketable?

– Were you FIXING / REPAIRING a problem or business pain? Helping to AVOID a problem or business pain? Or, were you helping to reach an ASPI-RATIONAL GOAL? In other words, helping to reach an articulated vision? (Typically, we do all 3, but one may be more evident.)

– What strengths were present? Are these examples of experiences where you lost yourself in your work and even lost track of time?

– Are there aspects of your work to which you were drawn that speak to your passions and interests (i.e. things that you can talk about for hours)?

– Can you learn from the negative aspect(s) of your stories? Are there experiences you're certain you don't want? Can that help you articulate what you would want instead?

– Are there themes in terms of the:
   ○ Process you used?
   ○ Functional expertise you offered?
   ○ Outcomes or impact you delivered?
   ○ Reason you were consistently selected over others?

– What impact did your efforts have on the organization / department / function / project? Was it the same contribution? Was it the same problem you were tasked with solving?

When you're at your best, what patterns exist? Note them here.

Related to Question #2: How will my PERSONAL PRIORITIES impact my next step?

– What were the environmental factors (e.g. culture) of the organization / business unit / function / department / team / taskforce? Is that important? The more completely you can pinpoint the environmental factors, the better. (See the Environmental Flourish Factors exercise in Chapter Three.)

– Are there patterns that speak to the leadership attitude of the organization? In other words, are they collaborative? Open to transformation? Focused on the means to end, rather than just the end result?

– What skills / expertise were you using? Does it represent what you like best about yourself?

– Which of your personal traits were evident? Are they consistent with the adjectives you'd use to describe yourself? (See the Characteristics and Traits exercise in Chapter Three.)

What are your top priorities? Note them here.

Related to Question #3: Who NEEDS what I have?

– In what function, role, or capacity were you serving? What was the structure (i.e. matrixed or traditional?) Are those factors important?

– In what industry were you working? Is that important?

– Where was the organization in its organizational lifecycle? Startup? Mature? Turnaround? Is that important?

– What was the size of the organization? Is that important?

– What was the organizational problem you were helping to solve? What value were you offering? In other words, what were you paid to deliver?

What are the patterns relative to each of these factors:

Industry:

Function:

Products / Services:

Size: Sales / Revenue:

Size (Employees):

Lifecycle:

Leadership Attitude /
Philosophy:

TIP

The size of the organization is usually an important factor, and one that is frequently overlooked. We'd recommend you look carefully at this question.

Just because you've worked for a medium sized company and a Fortune 50 company and been successful in both, doesn't mean that both represent the ideal environment for you, or the one in which you will add the most value.

For example, many divisions of Fortune 1000 companies function like small, entrepreneurial businesses.

Do you feel energized in an environment where you get to wear multiple hats and are a 'big fish in a small pond' having a bigger impact? If so, then a smaller company might be the ideal environment for you.

If, by contrast, you like the convenience of calling the Facilities Department when your office chair breaks rather than someone handing you a screwdriver, then a bigger company might be a better match.

This is a personal decision for each of us – there is no right or wrong.

Examining where you've been successful, happy, and had the most professional impact, is important.

Step Three

Do another quick review of the top 3 stories you've written and apply what we call the "Who, What, Where, When, Why, and How" test.

The goal of this is to examine your experiences from another perspective. Some of these might not be important to you, but it would helpful to explore.

- With whom were you doing this? Who were the people? What were their qualifications? Personalities? Values? etc.

- What specifically were you doing? And, for what purpose?

- Where were you doing it? Did the location matter? For instance, consider the geographic location or where within the organization you were working (headquarters, branch, etc.).

- When were you doing it? Where were you in your career? Did the timing matter?

- Why were you doing it and for what purpose? Was it tied to the organizational mission?

- How were you doing it?

The answers to these questions may not matter. If that's the case, it's okay. If they do matter, they're offering important insight into the nuances of what will create greater levels of satisfaction for you - your personal *Flourish Factor*.

Note your observations in the space below.

7. What is Your Best-Next-Step?

Let's check in with where we are.

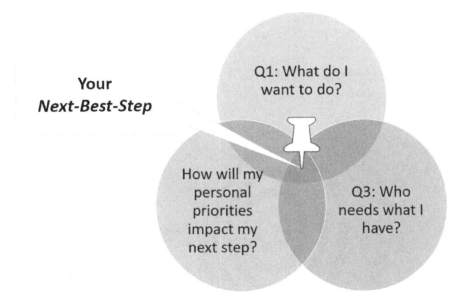

Your next-best-step is a confluence of your responses to the 3 core questions.

Now's the time to review your responses using the data you've synthesized in the *Flourish Factor* Profile and the Be a Better Storyteller exercise.

The time you take to develop clarity is a valuable gift you give yourself; you can't build a compelling message without that focus. As George Harrison once wrote: "If you don't know where you're going, any road will take you there."

In Chapter Four, we talked about 4 career options. Do you have clarity about which you're pursuing?

1) Current Profession / Current Industry

2) Different Profession / Current Industry

3) Current Profession / Different Industry

4) Different Profession / Different Industry

Which of your 2 or 3 possible options are viable based on your personal priorities and the needs of the marketplace?

Of the options, what are your answers to the following questions:

– What is your ideal role and can you articulate it?

– What qualifies you for this position?

– How do you differentiate yourself from your competition (e.g. knowledge, skills, expertise, credentials)?

– Can you articulate the business challenges you can help address?

Our goal is to help you identify your sweet spot, that is, the bulls-eye on your career dart board.

Source: Cliparts.co

What is your ideal role, based on the context of your personal priorities and the realities of the marketplace?

Keep in mind, the bulls-eye is at the center of the dartboard, but not everyone is able to hit the bulls-eye -- even if you're aimed at it and it's in focus.

The outer rings on the dartboard represent some other options you might consider.

Again, the *Flourish Factor* profile provides you with a baseline against which to evaluate opportunities and decide if an option is a good fit.

Taking the information from the *Flourish Factor* profile, let's consider those results in relation to the insights you gained in the Be a Better Storyteller exercise.

EXAMPLE:

A client with whom we worked, introduced himself as a sales guy, even though he was looking for something 'more.'

In other words, he had been very successful in the past in sales roles, but they hadn't really given him much satisfaction.

After working through the *Flourish Factor* and Be a Better Storyteller exercises, he came to realize why. Although he saw himself as a sales guy, his sweet spot was turning-around under performing businesses.

It turned out that he simply saw sales as a key factor in the turn-around / change management process.

Once he identified his sweet spot was serving as a change agent for under-performing businesses, he was able to pursue opportunities that were aligned.

The most important lesson was that he not only gained focus about what he wanted to pursue, he also understood why his previous roles were not satisfying.

Target Audience Profile

In the Be a Better Storyteller exercise, you were tracking patterns in your experiences. Those patterns were building a clearer picture of your audience -- of your bulls-eye. Now, let's get even more specific.

What organizations represent the kind of companies that:

1) Hire people to do the work you want to do?

2) Meet your *Flourish Factor* profile?

3) Align with your personal priorities?

Drawing on the work you completed in Chapter Six, build out this profile of your target audience.

Geography:

Industry:

Function:

Products / Services:

Size: Sales / Revenue:

Size (Employees):

Lifecycle:

Leadership Attitude /
Philosophy:

Other:

PART TWO:
FOCUS: Transitioning Clarity into Personal Branding

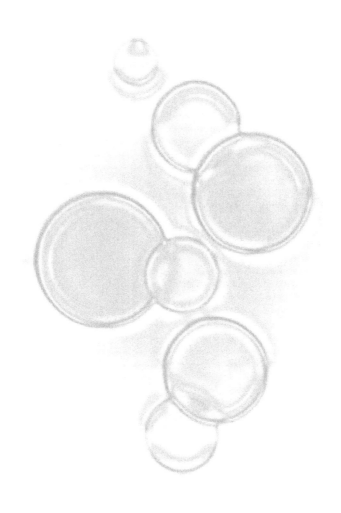

8. An Introduction to FOCUS: Transitioning Clarity into Personal Branding

Once you're clearer about the direction in which you want to go, it's time to craft your message.

The litmus test to determine if your messaging will actually hook your audience into a conversation -- is the ability to **paint a picture** of how you're a solution to their business' problem(s). In other words, can your target audience quickly visualize how you would add value in their organization?

EXAMPLE:

In a recent conversation with a manufacturing executive, he was able to quickly connect-the-dots of his Career Management Diagnostic to his audience's pain point.

He was in manufacturing and wanted to stay in manufacturing. Manufacturers in his geography were mature organizations.

From experience — which was then validated by his research, he identified that the pain or business problem is largely universal: needing to grow margins by making gains in efficiencies and netting cost improvements.

That happened to be his sweet spot. So, getting to his messaging was simpler.

END-TO-END MANUFACTURING EXECUTIVE
ELEVATE SUPPLY CHAIN PERFORMANCE | GROW MARGINS | APPLY LEAN

Hiring managers aren't looking to just fill an open requisition. The person they hope to hire must be able to address the specific concerns in their organization. In other words, they want to know who will make their lives easier.

For instance, if an organization is looking to hire a sales executive, they need someone who not only meets their position description requirements, but who can also address the "real" challenges they're experiencing.

To explain: they might need someone who can get all the members of the sales teams 'on the same page' and 'playing nicely together in the sandbox'. They might need someone expert at launching a new product or opening a new territory. Or, they may need someone to turn around an under-performing market that is affecting the overall financial results.

Your brand is **who you are in terms of where you add value**. It is not simply a list of your features. Your brand expresses how you are a solution to a business' problem(s).

That's where the *Flourish Factor* and Target Audiences profiles come in: they are the **ingredients to your branding message**.

How those ingredients are combined will form the foundation for your marketing collateral.

Your Bulls-Eye

In Chapter Seven, we introduced the concept of your bulls-eye. That is the sweet spot of your career dartboard. What's the bulls-eye on your dart board – the spot that represents your ideal target role? Remember, you're not being so specific as to say that the bulls-eye is the **only** option; there are other rings on the dartboard. However, your messaging needs to be targeted at the audience in the bulls-eye.

Source: Cliparts.co

For example, if a major cosmetic firm launches a luxury brand of mascara that retails at $45, they don't waste a dollar of their advertising budget marketing to the teenager who buys 99¢ mascara at a discount store. (Even though that teenager may save all their babysitting money to buy it).

The point is that your messaging needs to be targeted at the audience you're trying to attract, realizing that others may be drawn in as well.

That message can take various forms which may include a résumé / CV, commercial, bio, business cards, online profiles (e.g. LinkedIn, Twitter), etc.

To be clear, let's look at an example to show what we don't mean, and then what we do mean. A strong branding statement (in the form of a commercial) is the difference between saying:

I'm a sales executive with 25 years' experience.

Versus saying:

I'm a sales executive and what I do best is turn around under-performing markets and drive top-line growth.

The latter example shows how this person is a SOLUTION to the business problem.

The message is "This is where I'm an expert." Again, hiring managers want to hire the expert who can fix their specific problem.

Refer to the APPENDIX for a Case Study that further details this process.

Now the question is **how do you craft your own message**?

9. Branding Yourself: Crafting a Compelling Message

As you begin to craft your message, remember that you're focusing on WHO YOU ARE in terms of where you add value instead of "This is the job I want."

Your focus on your next-best-step is your BRAND ESSENCE.

How can you craft a message that is simple? Concise? And, easily understood by your audience?

Your message should:
- Speak to how you're a solution to a business problem
- Be clear language that reflects your communication style
- Be easy to remember and accurately repeatable

To better illustrate the process, we're going to walk you through a real-life example from one of our clients. We'll connect-the-dots by showing how the work he completed helped him gain clarity and focus, which created the foundation from which to build the messaging that helped him land a dream opportunity.

Connecting-the-Dots: Meet Phillipe

Phillipe, a supply chain executive with an international retail organization, was getting frustrated with his search, as he was responding to job postings and interviewing for roles that weren't a good fit. Either he ultimately wasn't interested, or he was interested, but not the top candidate.

Part of the problem was that he was defining himself based on the language of the job postings, rather than having a clear focus of the organizations challenges he was best at solving.

His target list consisted of retailers of similar size, but without consideration of whether they needed his particular expertise. It wasn't about his qualifications, it was about his messaging.

Phillipe's original messaging (from his résumé / CV summary) described his background and pedigree, but it didn't speak to his value-add.

Experienced Director of Supply Chain, Logistics and Operations. A dynamic and strategic thinker with a record of delivering results. Demonstrates performance in leading critical, enterprise-wide initiatives through strong collaboration, qualitative & quantitative decision-making and engaging talent management.

The message isn't poorly crafted, but it wasn't helping him hook his **desired target audience** into conversations.

So, how did we close the gap? We began by discussing the difference between Features and Benefits.

Features tell, while **Benefits sell.**

Perhaps this non-related example will explain that concept more fully. If when selling a new smartphone, the salesperson touts that it features a 20-megapixel camera, it will mean nothing if the buyer isn't technical. Instead, if the salesperson says that phone features a 20-megapixel camera which means you can take a photo with your phone and enlarge it to poster size with crystal-clear clarity, then the **benefit** of that feature becomes clearer.

How did we apply that concept to Phillipe's situation? We asked the "So What?" question to drive his responses into focus.

For example, when he described "leading critical, enterprise-wide initiatives" was a feature but it didn't explain how that added value to the organization.

We dug into that concept more fully by asking "So what? Where did that add value to the organization?"

Bolstered by the data from his *Flourish Factor* profile and the Be a Better Storyteller exercise, he was able to answer it this way:

Leading the critical, enterprise-wide initiatives meant that I was able to gain strong organizational buy-in to drive change amidst complex logistical needs that were in constant flux. In other words, we'd set a direction and a then there would be another shift in the market that would mean we'd have to pivot in response in order to stay relevant and competitive.

A note on process: you must first be able to get to your value-add before you can polish it. Another way to think of this is: **What are the end results of what you do that can be seen or touched?**

Here is his branding statement as it appeared on his résumé:

SUPPLY CHAIN EXECUTIVE
EVOLVE SCM INTO COMPETITIVE ADVANTAGE BY OPTIMIZING VALUE CHAIN

We were able to get to his value-add quickly as it was the pattern that emerged from his Be a Better Storyteller exercise. It helped expand his focal point and "see the patterns in the crop circles."

This was the new summary from his résumé / CV. There are core ideas that carried over from his original (or before) messaging, but now served to hook his audience into conversations.

SUPPLY CHAIN EXECUTIVE
EVOLVE SCM INTO COMPETITIVE ADVANTAGE BY OPTIMIZING VALUE CHAIN

Build shared vision, gaining strong buy-in to drive change amidst complex growing and shifting logistics needs. Lead-by- example, curate and develop strong, diverse teams that deliver exceptional performance through inevitable ups-and- downs of market cycles.

Exceptionally skilled at optimizing value by building strong coalitions of key stakeholders and leveraging institutional knowledge to drive margin improvement.

Leverage global supply chain strategies that achieved sustainable cost reductions, significant customer service improvements, increased (high) inventory turn rates, and minimized distribution and transportation costs.

As a result, Phillipe landed his ideal role by clearly articulating how he was a solution to a business problem. Specifically, "to drive change amidst complex growing and shifting logistics needs."

There were other candidates with similar qualifications, but he hooked his audience into the conversation (which is where the hiring decision is made) by addressing their specific needs (i.e. pain point).

No other candidate got to the heart of the matter as directly as he did. He quickly became the 'best fit' candidate and received a highly competitive offer.

How do you know if the messaging is on target? This is the litmus test:

 – Does it speak to how you're a solution to a business problem(s)

 – Can you articulate the challenges your target organizations are facing.

10. Conclusion

In conclusion, this clarification process takes time and a willingness to expend the energy necessary to determine your focus. As we said earlier, it's a valuable gift you give yourself to determine your next-best-step.

As we reviewed Phillipe's example, it may have seemed simple, but in fact, he put more than 8-hours of effort into completing the exercises and researching his audience.

However, when his networking efforts became more fruitful because he was having conversations with business leaders who needed what he had to offer, he knew he was on the right track.

That effort was rewarded when he landed his ideal role where he loves what he does, he's appreciated, and gets to be his best-self at work. He thought the time and effort were well worth it.

Is it worth it to you?

APPENDIX

We wanted to provide additional resources to guide this process. We hope you will find the examples and tools helpful.

S-T-A-R-S Story Template

Describe the scope or problem **S (Scope)**	
Explain the task ... what was your challenge and / or why it was so important **T (Task)**	
List the specific actions to show you how you resolved the problem **A (Action)**	
What was the result or accomplishment and what were the benefits? Can the result be quantified or qualified? **R (Result)**	
Why did it matter? What skills were you using? What traits and strengths did you employ? **S (Significance)**	

Other Ways to Identify Strengths

When building your personal brand, it helps to know what your strengths are and when you use them. As noted in Chapter Two, being able to leverage strengths every day at work will help ensure you flourish in your new environment.

About strengths, Debra and Danielle are both huge fans of the Gallup StrengthsFinder 2.0 tool. By purchasing a new copy of the book or e-book called *StrengthsFinder 2.0* by Tom Rath, you can gain access to the tool.

Action Verbs

As a storyteller, it is important that you describe your experience in terms that are as powerful as possible. The following list of Action Verbs is a tool to help get you thinking about the skills you've used and the impact you've offered.

NOTE: When crafting your marketing collateral, such as your Résumé / CV, each bullet should start with an action verb. Review the list below and highlight actions you've taken.

When I've worked with PEOPLE, I have...		
Adapted	Influenced	Represented
Addressed	Initiated	Requested
Administered	Inspired	Rescued
Advised	Instructed	Resolved
Assessed	Justified	Restructured
Assisted	Learned	Resurrected
Calibrated	Led	Rethought
Coached	Managed	Revamped
Collaborated	Masterminded	Reversed
Communicated	Maximized	Revitalized
Conceived	Mentored	Scheduled
Conducted	Motivated	Segmented
Consulted	Orchestrated	Served
Counseled	Outperformed	Shared
Decided	Partnered	Showed
Delegated	Performed	Solved
Demonstrated	Persistently pursued	Spearheaded
Determined	Persuaded	Spurred growth
Directed	Pioneered	Stabilized
Eliminated	Practiced	Staffed
Enforced	Presented	Strengthened
Established	Produced	Supervised
Expedited	Professionalized	Taught
Facilitated	Projected	Tended
Galvanized	Protected	Tested
Garnered	Provided	Trained
Guided	Reconciled	Triumphed
Handpicked	Recruited	Other:
Hired	Reduced	Other
When I've worked with DATA, I have...		
Administered	Determined	Read
Analyzed	Developed	Recorded
Arranged	Edited	Reconciled

Assembled	Evaluated	Refined
Assessed	Formulated	Reorganized
Authored	Identified	Reported
Balanced	Integrated	Researched
Budgeted	Interpreted	Revised
Calculated	Marketed	Setup
Co-authored	Modified	Simplified
Compiled	Organized	Sorted
Completed	Planned	Standardized
Composed	Presented	Streamlined
Computed	Processed	Systematized
Condensed	Promoted	Synthesized
Converted	Programmed	Tracked
Coordinated	Proved	Updated
Corrected	Provided	Verified
Defined	Publicized	Wrote
Designed	Published	Other:

When I've worked with
PRODUCTS, SERVICES, or OPERATIONS, I have…

Arranged	Expanded	Originated
Assembled	Fabricated	Persistently pursued
Balanced	Formed	Pioneered
Bargained	Founded	Presented
Built	Garnered	Produced
Centralized	Generated	Professionalized
Conceived	Guided	Purchased / Procured
Conserved	Handled	Reconstructed
Consolidated	Improved	Redesigned
Constructed	Innovated	Reduced
Converted	Inspected	Repaired
Created	Installed	Rescued
Cut costs	Introduced	Restructured
Demonstrated	Invented	Revitalized
Designed	Masterminded	Reversed
Determined	Modernized	Shaped
Developed	Opened	Strengthened
Devised	Operated	Tended
Eliminated	Orchestrated	Tested
Established	Organized	Upgraded

Visualizing Your Skills
(Extension of Marketable / Transferrable Skills)

If you're struggling at all with the results of the Marketable / Transferrable Skills exercise, it may be helpful to use the following quadrant to help visualize and sort those skills.

High Skill / High Interest	High Skill / Low Interest
(Pursue / Be Your Best Self at Work)	(Burn-out area / You're in a rut)
Low Skill / High Interest	**Low Skill / Low Interest**
(Possible focus for Professional Growth and / or Areas for Development)	(Don't waste your time / Stop doing them)

Additional Before + After Examples

The process of branding yourself means that you'll be narrowing the focus of your job search in order to increase your appeal to your audience.

Here are additional examples of strong branding statements, which include the different formats of marketing collateral (i.e. Resume / CV, elevator pitch) in which you would use your branding statement.

Think of it this way, a well-crafted branding statement is – at the same time – specific in its value-add while being broad in its appeal.

1) This is an example of a BEFORE COMMERCIAL / ELEVATOR PITCH for an attorney who was looking to make a shift in his career:

> Former in-house counsel with significant experience in contract negotiations, contract drafting, litigation management, and complex transactions management. Served as mediator in foreclosure and business disputes. Represented employer in mediations. Interested in mediating commercial disputes. Also interested in providing business legal services.

Here is his AFTER COMMERCIAL / ELEVATOR PITCH. Notice how he is describing himself based on how he wants others to know and understand his value. This is a more forward-looking perspective in his messaging:

> Impartial and skilled mediator, expert at resolving commercial disputes while avoiding expensive litigation, negative publicity, and protracted drains on organizational time, money, and productivity.

2. This next example is also a COMMERCIAL / ELEVATOR PITCH, but it's done in a more conversational style.

The executive was targeting the board members at start-up high tech companies that are launching never-before-seen technologies. Think about those companies striving to be the next Facebook, or tech-genius who wants to be the next Mark Zuckerberg.

In the example, notice how he includes their pain-point; that is, he knows they're likely struggling with making sure that the revenue they're generating is making it through to the bottom-line.

> As a COO, I'm looking to connect with high-tech organizations launching never-before-seen technologies and are poised on the precipice of hyper-growth. I'm best at aligning strategies and tactics that ensure what hits the top-line makes it to the bottom-line.

3) In this example from a Business Development and Sales executive's Résumé / CV, we can see how the branding statement is explained or unpacked in the PROFILE / SUMMARY.

BUSINESS DEVELOPMENT AND SALES LEADER

Create New Revenue Streams | Develop and Commercialize New Product Applications

Commercialize new products and generate demand by identifying business needs or market opportunities; develop product solutions meeting demand. Proactively manage cross-functional development teams, creating solutions. Negotiate customer-unique complex contracts reflecting functional value rather than price per unit.

Evolve customers from transactional sales relationships to trusted partners through in-depth penetration of target customers. Cultivate trusted relationships creating "win-win" high value sales opportunities through unique offerings.

Sales Management | Product & Partnership Development | Business Analysis

Profit Maximization | Financial Acumen (CPA)

---

4) Because LinkedIn has become the "employment hunting ground," it's critical to have a strong presence.

Even when you're gainfully employed, your LinkedIn headline should never read your title at XX Company, but should include language about how you add value.

Here is an example of a LINKEDIN HEADLINE for a Senior Vice President of Operations:

> Senior VP, Operations: Refine Operational Strategy | Improve Competitive Positioning | Maximize Stakeholder Value

5) In our final example, we're again showing a RÉSUMÉ / CV PROFILE / SUMMARY so you can see the branding message and how it's built.

This is an example from a Chief Human Resource Officer (CHRO) who landed his best-fit role after the CEO saw his messaging. The CEO was seeking a partner who understood and could apply LEAN principles.

She wanted an HR partner who was well-versed in applying and understanding LEAN principles, as the departing HR executive was not and that was impeding progress.

ENGAGEMENT-FOCUSED HR EXECUTIVE

Solve Complex Enterprise Issues | Create Culture of Resilience | Apply LEAN which Maximizes Results

Thought-Leader passionate about navigating broad-scale, organizational change through the application of LEAN methodologies. Thrive in environments where pushing the boundaries of conventional thinking is the norm and breakthrough innovations lead the way through market shifts and transformation.

Employ evidence-based practice to align HR priorities to business strategy. Drive company results and engagement by developing resilience, focus, and self-awareness in staff and leaders. Offer multi-industry, global experience. Multilingual: Spanish & French.

Talent Management | Organizational Design & Development | Executive Coaching

360° & Behavioral Assessments | Employee & Labor Relations | Business Process Redesign

---

A Case Study of Coachable Moments

With all our combined years of coaching, there are some stories that stand the test of time and illustrate the ideas we've laid out in the book.

Here's another scenario that portrays how one client used the information of the 3 Questions to help her identify and land her best-next-step -- within 2-months.

Meet a Director of Corporate Tax and follow the trail of her answers to the career management diagnostic questions:

1) What do I want to do?

*She wanted to continue in a similar role, in a similar industry. When we dug deeper into that looking at where she was at her best and where she added the most value (they were the same thing, by the way), she wanted to **minimize tax liability for the corporation, enhance their tax planning capabilities to drive compliance, and control the cost of compliance**. That was her focus.*

2) How will my personal priorities impact my next step?

She wanted to work another 5- to 7-years before retiring. Luckily, in her geography, there were plenty of large employers in her same industry with roles like her most recent role, but not necessarily openings at that moment.

The 2 biggest drivers for this client were to match or increase her previous compensation package, and to find an organization with the 'right' leadership attitude.

3) Who needs what I have? *Through her research, she determined any organization in her industry would need what she has to offer. The critical difference came to the 2nd part of the question: who was the stakeholder for whom that issue is causing insomnia?*

*This Director of Corporate Tax wanted an organization whose leadership (and their attitude) was looking for **out-of-the-box solutions to help enhance their tax planning capabilities**. That would be an example of the business pain she fixed.*

To be clear, she wasn't looking for a company that wanted someone to come in, sit down, shut-up, and simply do what they were told.

In her prior roles, she created tax compliance tools that quickly generated "what-if" scenarios that evaluated multiple tax positions.

Those scenarios gave the organizational leaders the decision-grade data they needed to respond to complex changes in tax regulations -- which saved money and reduced exposure.

She wanted to do that for another organization whose C-level officers were looking for that kind of expertise.

Together, we built this profile of her target audience:

Organizational Profile	
Industry:	*Pharmaceutical / Biotech*
Size:	*+5K employees*
Lifecycle:	*Organization: Mature but growing; mid-stage in high-growth*
Geography:	*80 km / 50 mi radius of personal postal code*
Products / Services:	*Rx or OTC (Over the counter) products*
Revenue:	*$1B+*
Leadership Attitude:	*Seeking an internal tax expert to present out-of-the-box solutions to help enhance their tax planning capabilities*
Business Problem:	*Need better options regarding tax compliance and cost of compliance to impact profitability*

Next, we profiled the ultimate stakeholder(s) for whom that issue is causing insomnia, which she identified as C-level officers of an organization.

This is important to note, as a director, she didn't report to the C-level officer, she reported to an SVP who was 2 levels below.

But the stake holder to whom she needed to appeal was the person being held accountable for the organization's financial results.

Armed with this information, she built a list of the organizations she wanted to target, the names of the stakeholders, and crafted a plan to reach them. She landed an ideal role within 2 months.

12-Month Career Checklist

"If you are not actively managing your own career,
no one else is doing it for you."

– Danielle + Debra)

As an ongoing exercise, you should be reflecting on your career – whether it's because your annual performance review is due, that you've landed a new role, or want to more proactively manage your career going forward.

Making time to proactively manage your career is a valuable gift you can give yourself. We recommend setting a 30-minute appointment with yourself each month to attend to your own career management. (NOTE: If you move the appointment for convenience, track if you change the date and time more than 3-times. If so, ask yourself: ***When am I going to make my sustainable employability a top priority?)***

This checklist can be used when starting a new role (start with Month 1), or can be aligned to a calendar-year schedule (start with Month 12).

Month	Action Steps
Month #1	If starting a new role, pay attention to the keys to your success. If planning for the start of the new year, consider adapting these ideas to give yourself a fresh perspective on your position: 1) Learning the new role and being clear about expectations (keep up with the learning curve, listening instead of talking, operating from assumption that there is information you don't have) 2) Gaining boss' support (be clear about expectations and communication preferences) 3) Building strong internal coalitions (but being careful not to trust too fast until you learn the political landscape) 4) Go slow in order to go fast (be open to new ideas, owning what you don't know in a new organization / landscape, recognizing that being new gives you latitude to ask questions no one else may be able to ask)

Month #2   Ask yourself:
1) What are my expectations in this role? Do I have anticipated goals or milestones I'm targeting? Have projects / promotions been promised to me? Do I have a reminder in my calendar to check in about their status?
2) What's at least one S-T-A-R-S Story I can document this month that personifies my brand / shows where I add value?
3) Have I updated my personal webpage this month? If I'm using Twitter, is it linked? Am I tweeting quality content?

Month #3   Be honest when you ask yourself:
1) What have I done for my own networking? Did I go to lunch with a colleague outside my work circle? Outside my function / industry? Remember, as career management expert Robin Greenspan said so eloquently, **"It's easier to network, than need-work."**
2) Have I updated LinkedIn this month? Have I posted any status updates or shared links with my contacts? Have I grown my network?

Month #4   In terms of the time you're committing to your career management efforts, have you:
1) Looked at any job leads lately? If you were suddenly unemployed tomorrow, are you a qualified and desirable candidate for any positions you'd be targeting? If there are gaps in your skills / expertise / training / certifications, the time to know that is now when you can actively fill that gap while you're working.
2) Recorded at least one S-T-A-R-S Story you can document this month that personifies your personal brand / shows where you add value?

Month #5   Managing your own sustainable employability means that you keep up with your professional development. Ask yourself:
1) What have I done for my professional development this month? What will I commit to completing by next month?
2) Have I updated my LinkedIn profile this month? Have I posted any status updates or shared links with my contacts?
3) Have I grown my network?

Month #6	Taking into account the milestones you articulated in month #2, have you assessed your progress toward them? Ask yourself: 1) Am I on course? If yes, do I need to stretch myself further? 2) Have I met them? If so, what are new goals / objectives? If not, why have I not met them? What's getting in the way? How can I remove those obstacles?
Month #7	Reflecting should be a part of this process 1) What's the reality of the state of your role? Often times when a situation deteriorates, it happens gradually. 2) Refer back to the In-Demand Skills exercise to assess yourself against the market. 3) What articles or resources have you read about the state of your industry?
Month #8	Ask yourself: 1) What have I done for my own networking? Did I go to lunch with a colleague outside my work circle? Outside my function / industry? 2) What exposure have I gained in social media this month? Have I been active on LinkedIn? Are there other sites where I see other professionals in my field congregating? Have I Googled to see if there are any industry niche sites where I should have a presence?
Month #9	1) What's one S-T-A-R-S Story I can document this month that personifies my personal branding statement? 2) Refer back to the Be a Better Storyteller exercise. Are there new emerging patterns in the S-T-A-R-S stories you have been recording.
Month #10	Ask yourself: 1) Managing my own sustainable employability means that I keep up with my professional development. What have I done for my professional development this month? Are there any conference, trade shows, or professional networking events I can attend in person to get face-time with key industry decision makers? 2) Are there community efforts in which I could engage that would get me out and interacting with more / different people while giving something back to a cause or the community?

Month #11	Check in with yourself:
	1) What have I missed in prior months' check-ups? Can I finish them or plan for them now?
	2) What's my pitch for networking, especially around the holidays or key life events? When someone says, "So tell me about yourself…" how will I answer? Will I respond with my title, selling the company for which I work, or will I respond with my brand to showcase who I am?

Month #12	Conduct a year-end review:
	1) Where did I do a good job managing my career? How do I make sure I build on that success next year?
	2) How has my stress level changed this past year? Is it escalating? Where are there gaps? What will I do to close them?
	3) Have I revisited the exercises in this book to either review my results or update them?

Networking Tips

– Remember, networking is about relationships. Listen more than you talk.

– When networking, look for people who are, or can be your advocates -- in addition to your direct supervisor.

– Network outside the company / organization and outside your own industry. Expanding connections will help provide perspective and possible insight into other opportunities.

– Share best practices with contacts in similar roles in different organizations or industries as it helps to build your personal brand and demonstrates your value as a professional.

– Opportunities are connected to people, so fostering relationships will serve you well.

– Reciprocate. Look for ways to proactively share information with your network.

– A basic tenant of networking is that people hire those they know, like, and trust.

ABOUT THE AUTHORS

Danielle Beauparlant Moser and **Debra Fehr Heindel** are Career Management advocates and Practice Leaders of blt Careers, a boutique executive coaching firm built almost solely from referrals from highly-satisfied clients. Their passion is helping people lead better lives through work.

Along with their private practice, Danielle and Debra have been affiliated with global talent management firms since the early 1990s working with clients across all industries. They write prolifically on career development and management practices.

As career management leaders, they were pioneers in the expansion of blended learning and virtual delivery.

Having both lived and worked internationally, they coach clients across a variety of professions and industries, working with professionals who are located across the globe.

Danielle resides in Asheville, NC with her husband, two daughters, and three rescue dogs. Debra lives in Fort Worth, Texas with her husband, Mal and border collie, Chloe.

As Debra and Danielle often tell people, life's too short for work to stink!

For information and other resources or to contact Danielle or Debra go to:

www.bltcareers.com

https://twitter.com/bltcareers (@bltCareers)

Made in the USA
Columbia, SC
08 April 2019